Numeracy for Childcare Students

A Basic Skills Guide

Excellence in Childcare
Series Editor: Maureen Smith

This book is part of the Excellence in Childcare Series. The series is designed to support students and NVQ candidates, practitioners, managers and trainers to develop their skills and offer a high quality service to children and families.

Books in the series are written by experts with many years' experience of and commitment to the childcare sector. As the sector grows and develops, there is a demand not only for more childcare provision, but for better quality provision. The sector now requires very well qualified, excellent practitioners who can support children's development throughout the preschool years. The series aims to help new and established practitioners become confident, imaginative, excellent professionals.

Numeracy for Childcare Students

A Basic Skills Guide

June Green

 David Fulton Publishers

David Fulton Publishers Ltd
The Chiswick Centre, 414 Chiswick High Road, London W4 5TF

www.fultonpublishers.co.uk

First published in Great Britain by David Fulton Publishers 2003

Note: the right of June Green to be identified as the author of this work has been asserted by her in accordance with the Copyright, Designs and Patents Act 1988.

David Fulton Publishers is a division of Granada Learning Limited, part of Granada plc.

British Library Cataloguing in Publication Data
A catalogue record for this book is available from the British Library.

ISBN 1–84312–024–0

Typeset by FiSH Books, London
Printed and bound in Great Britain by Ashford Colour Press, Gosport, Hants.

Contents

This book is dedicated
to my Godson, Corran McGarvey

Acknowledgements

Thanks again to my son Radley for his valuable input to this book, for testing out the activities and for giving an honest opinion!

Thank you to Gail Blackwood for taking valuable time to read through these numeracy books and being friend enough to be honest with me.

Thanks to Steve Lee, Trish Jacobs (who still makes me laugh) and Susan Lewinson for their support and patience.

Thanks to all in the Early Years, Care and Public Services Department at South Birmingham College for their encouragement.

Thanks to all at David Fulton who have been a part of this Basic Skills series, for their patience, good humour, advice and encouragement. Special mention to Anne Summers who always cheers me up when she phones. It's been a great experience working with you.

Introduction

Welcome to *Numeracy for Childcare Students: A Basic Skills Guide* workbook.

I take it that since you are reading this you are doing a childcare course with basic skills added in. How do you feel about it? So many students' reaction is OH NO, NOT MATHS!, or they get really worried by it, while others get bored. I can understand that. However, the numeracy course that you are doing is not like the maths you did at school. Wherever possible it is related to or linked into childcare; where not it is linked into everyday life. Some of the activities are fun, for example where you time each other putting a nappy on!

So what is this book for? The book contains some activities linked to each of the sessions of your course. You can use it in different ways; if you find yourself speeding along in class you can use the activities to build on your learning, or to work independently. If there is something you are finding hard to understand, use the activities to help you or just use them for fun things to do! At the top of each page there is a box like this:

> **This activity relates to:**
> **Entry level one, session 2**

The box tells you the level and session to which the activity relates. You will be able to monitor your own progress through the levels.

There are sections in this book that contain

- a glossary of words used in maths;
- 'mental maths strategies';
- space for you to record the weekly maths quiz; and
- a section for you to record the meanings of any new maths vocabulary you come across.

Glossary

While doing the numeracy course you are likely to come across some unfamiliar terms. In order to help you, here is a list of the main numeracy terms and what they mean. Turn to this page whenever you come across an unfamiliar word, and return to it whenever necessary to until you know the meaning off by heart.

There will be many more terms as you go through the course, but you will understand them better if you find out their meanings as you use them. There is a blank page after the glossary for you to write in new words and their meanings as you come across them.

Calculate

Using your knowledge of number systems and the way they work to find the answer to a sum/number problem.

Data

Information made up of facts, statistics, measurements and so on.

Decimal

A fraction in which a decimal point (a dot) is followed by numbers that represent tens, hundredths, thousandths.

Digit

A written symbol that represents any number from 0–9.

Metric

A measurement relating to the metric system (e.g. gram, millimetre).

Table

A set of figures or information arranged in columns and rows.

Students' glossary

This page is for you to write in new words and their meanings as you come across them.

Mental maths strategies

On the next few pages you will find some ways to improve mental maths. These strategies will help you to develop your mental calculations.

Every so often your tutor will give you a mental maths quiz to keep you on your toes. You will be able to use and practise these strategies and find the ones that work best for you. You will probably develop some of your own – that's OK as long as they show you the right answers.

After the mental maths strategies there are some blank pages for you to record your answers to these quizzes. This will help you to keep track of your progress.

How you use the strategies is up to you. I suggest that you read through the strategy, then practise the task that is given. As you get better at it ask your friends and family to help you out by giving you some mental maths tasks to do, perhaps while you are washing up. It helps the time go faster! As you become more confident make the tasks harder and remember that *'little and often is better than lots now and then'*.

Have fun!

Mental addition

Some of the strategies for mental addition are very similar to using a counting line. Here are some to try.

1. Put the larger number first and then count on, for example 3 + 10 = 10 + 3; count on 3 from 10 and you get to 13.

   Try these:
   * 6 + 9
   * 7 + 10

2. Split numbers up and then add them together, for example 40 + 15 = 40 + 10 + 5, and you get 55.

   Try these:
   * 32 + 16
   * 44 + 23

3. Count on in 10s, for example 33 + 24 = 33 + 20 + 4 = 57.

   Try these:
   • 12 + 45
   • 20 + 53

4. Break both numbers into 10s and units, for example 34 + 25 = 30 + 20 + 4 + 5 = 59.

   Try these:
   • 15 + 23
   • 42 + 12

5. To add single digits, mentally pair numbers together to make them easier to add; for example, in 3 + 5 + 6 + 4 + 7 the 6 and the 4 make 10 and the 7 and the three make 10. Therefore you have 10 + 10 + 5. It's better isn't it? The answer is 25.

   Try these:
   • 6 + 2 + 7 + 4 + 3
   • 9 + 4 + 2 + 8 + 1

6. To add two-digit numbers mentally pair together units and 10s to make them easier to add together, for example, in 46 + 32 + 54 + 71 the 70 and the 30 make 100, the 50 and the 40 make 90, the 6 and the 4 make 10, so you have 100 + 90 +10 + 2 + 1 = 203.

   Try these:
   • 86 + 34 + 56
   • 91 + 54 + 12 + 36

7. Recognise patterns, for example 6 + 3 = 9; 16 + 3 + 19; 26 + 3 = 29 and so on.

   Try completing these patterns:

• 2 + 9 = 11	•
• 12 + 9 = 21	•
•	• 26 + 4 = 30
•	•
•	•
•	• 56 + 4 = 60

As you start to work with larger numbers you need to simply extend the strategy to use 100, 1000 and so on.
Make sure you can do it with the lower numbers first though.

Mental subtraction

1. Count forward from the smaller number, for example 24 – 13 = 13 to 20 is 7, 20 to 24 is 4, add 7 and 4 and you get 11. 24 –13 = 11.

   Try these:
   • 28 – 15
   • 44 – 13

2. Count forward from the smallest number in 10s and 1s; for example, 66 – 41 = 41 to 50 is 9, 50 to 60 is 10, 60 to 66 is 6. Add 9, 10 and 6 together and you get 25. The answer is 66 – 41 = 25.

   Try these:
   • 74 – 32
   • 95 – 46

3. Count forward from the smallest number in 1s and 10s; for example, 53 – 26 = 26 to 30 is 4, 30 to 40 is 10, 40 to 50 is 10, 50 to 53 is 3. Add 4, 10,10 and 3 together and you get 27. The answer is 53 – 26 = 27.

   Try these:
   • 37 – 9
   • 54 – 36

4. Splitting numbers into 10s and units, for example, 89 – 43 = 89 – 40 = 49, 49 – 3 = 46. The answer is 46

   Try these:
   • 76 – 29
   • 92 – 53

5. Recognising patterns as with addition; for example,
   34 – 9 = 25
   44 – 9 = 35
   54 – 9 = 45

   Try completing these:

• 66 – 5 = 61	• 9 – 5 = 4
•	•
• 86 – 5 = 81	• 29 – 5 = 24
•	•
•	•

As you start to work with larger numbers you need to simply extend the strategy to use 100s, 1000s and so on.
Make sure you can do it with the lower numbers first though.

Mental multiplication

1. To multiply by two just double the digit; for example, $2 \times 2 = 4$.

2. To multiply a double digit by 2, double the 10s, double the units and add together; for example, $2 \times 22 = 2 \times 20 = 40$, $2 \times 2 = 4$, $40 + 4 = 44$. **Answer is 44.**

   Try these:
   - 2×6
   - 2×10
   - 2×31
   - 2×24

2. To multiply by 4, double it and double it again; for example, $4 \times 10 = 2 \times 10 = 20$, $2 \times 20 = 40$. **Answer is 40.**

   Try these:
   - 4×22
   - 4×8
   - 4×9
   - 4×3
   - 4×21

3. To multiply by 5, multiply by 10 and halve your answer; for example, $5 \times 5 = 5 \times 10 = 50$ divided by $2 = 25$. **Answer is 25.**

   Try these:
   - 5×10
   - 5×6
   - 5×9
   - 5×8
   - 5×7

4. Use near round numbers and adjust the answer; for example, $3 \times 9 = 3 \times 10 = 30 - 3 = 27$. **Answer is 27.**

   Try these:
   - 4×8
   - 3×4
   - 5×9
   - 7×8

5. Split numbers and multiply each part; for example, $2 \times 72 = 2 \times (70 + 2) = (2 \times 70) + (2 \times 2) = 140 + 4 = 144$. **Answer is 144.**

   Try these:
   - 3×23
   - 4×15
   - 5×61
   - 10×12

Mental division

1. When you want to divide by 2, halve the number; for example, $6 \div 2 = 3$. **Answer is 3.**

   Try these:
   - $10 \div 2$
   - $28 \div 2$
   - $44 \div 2$
   - $86 \div 2$

2. To divide a double digit number by 2, split the number and halve each digit; for example, $36 \div 2 =$ half of 30 plus half of $6 = 15 + 3 = 18$. **Answer is 18.**

   Try these:
   - $88 \div 2$
   - $64 \div 2$
   - $46 \div 2$
   - $42 \div 2$

3. When you want to divide by 4, halve the number and then halve it again; for example, $12 \div 4 = 12 \div 2 = 6 \div 2 = 3$. **Answer is 3.**

   Try these:
   - $34 \div 4$
   - $48 \div 4$
   - $62 \div 4$
   - $82 \div 4$

4. Break the calculation into parts; for example, $90 \div 6 = (90 \div 3) \div 2 = 30 \div 2 = 15$. **Answer is 15.**

   Try these:
   - $34 \div 4$
   - $60 \div 12$
   - $84 \div 4$
   - $96 \div 6$
   - $120 \div 4$

That's the end of the mental maths strategies.

It's important to remember that you can use combinations of these methods when doing the more complicated equations.

Mental maths quiz

These pages are for you to keep a record of your mental maths quizzes.

Date

Date

Date

Date

Date

Date

Date

Date

Date

Date

Date

Date

Date

Date

Date

Date

Date

Date

Date

Date

Date

Date

Date

Date

Entry level one activities

These activities relate to:
Entry level one, session 1

Activity 1

In session 1 you looked at different ways numbers can be written in **digits** and **words**.

Make an A3-size poster for someone who is learning about numbers. It should include the following:

⇨ The digit
⇨ The word
⇨ All numbers up to 20.
⇨ What the number means, e.g.

Activity 2

We also looked at the order of numbers using a number line:

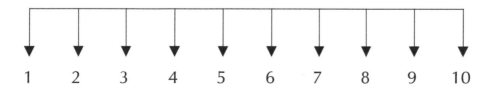

Work out the answers to the following questions using the counting line:

⇨ Sam is 5 years old; how old was he three years ago?
⇨ Annie will be 9 in four years' time; how old is she now?

⇨ Trish and Steve have three children: Joey is 5 years old, Laura is 3, Susan is 1. Work out the answers to the following questions about the children and then check them using the counting line.
- How much older is Joey than Laura and Susan?
- How much younger is Susan than Joey and Laura?
- How much older is Laura than Susan?
- How much younger is Laura than Joey?

> **These activities relate to:**
> **Entry level one, session 2**

Activity 1

REMINDER!
Ordinal numbers are the numbers we use to put things in numerical order. A digit or a word can represent ordinal numbers, but the number has something added to it. What is it? Look back to handout '*ORDERING ORDINALS*', from session 2, to give you some help.

In session 2 you worked on **ordinal numbers**. Look at the results of the egg-and-spoon race that are written below. Put the children into their positions in the table.

- Surjit was number 4 over the finishing line.
- Radley was number 1 over the finishing line.
- Daniel was number 3 over the finishing line.
- Chris was number 6 over the finishing line.
- June was last over the finishing line.
- Sheila was number 2 over the finishing line.
- Jack was number 5 over the finishing line.

Postion	Name
1st	
2nd	
3rd	
4th	
5th	
6th	
7th	

These activities relate to:
Entry level one, session 2

Activity 2

In session 2 you also looked at different ways of **writing** numbers; for example, Roman numerals and Arabic numerals:

I	1
II	2
III	3

Using the pictures on this page and the next, make an A3-size poster to show the numbers 1–5 in Arabic and Roman numerals.

This activity relates to:
Entry level one, session 3

In session 3 you looked at **addition** and **subtraction** using numbers up to 10.

Below are some addition and subtraction calculations and their answers. Can you match the calculation to the answer?

10 − 6 =

⊘⊘⊘⊘⊘ − ⊘⊘ =

| 7 |

9 − 2 =

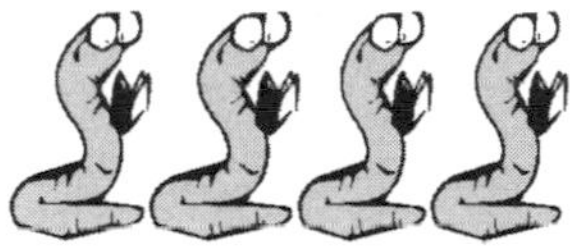

| 8 |

| 6 |

take away 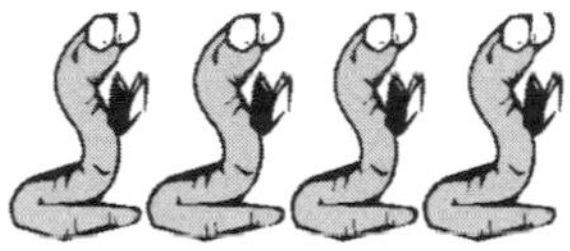   leaves

| 10 |

7 + 3 =

| 7 |

♦ ♦ ♦ ♦ + ♦ ♦ ♦ =

| 0 |

5 + 1 =

| 3 |

add   =

| 4 |

These activities relate to:
Entry level one, session 4

In session 4 you worked on completing calculations using a **calculator**.

Activity 1

Draw a line from the number/symbol to its button on the calculator.

9   1

5   3

7   0

2   8

×   ÷

−   +

4   =

6   •

Activity 2

Below is Damien's maths test. Check the answers on a calculator. Correct the answers he got wrong.

7 + 3 = 10	6 + 2 = 7	7 + 1 = 8
10 − 6 = 4	5 − 1 = 4	8 − 3 = 6
7 + 1 = 9	6 − 3 = 3	8 − 2 = 5
8 − 4 = 3	5 + 2 = 7	3 + 6 = 9

These activities relate to:
Entry level one, session 5

Activity 1

One of the things you looked at in session 5 was **money** and the different coins and notes we use.

Below are some prices. Which notes and coins could you use to make up the money?

£3.10 ....

75p ....

48p ....

£1.50 ....

£6.10 ....

Activity 2

Another topic you looked at was maths terminology: smaller than, bigger than.

Below are some shapes for you to put in order of size. Put the first ones into largest to smallest and the second set into smallest to largest.

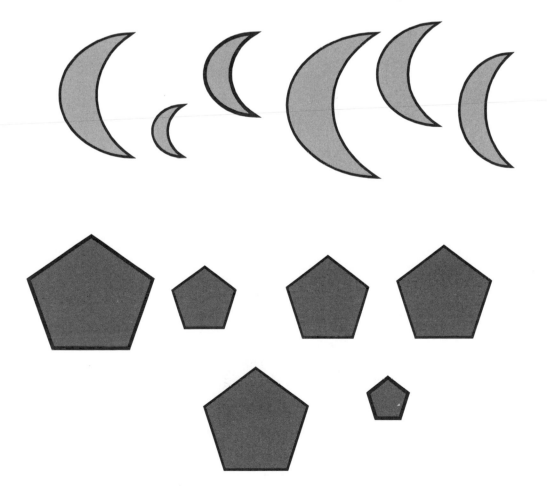

**This activity relates to:
Entry level one, session 6**

In session 6 you covered some more terminology.
Below are some questions for you to answer.

1. Which child is the shortest?

2. Which baby is the heaviest?

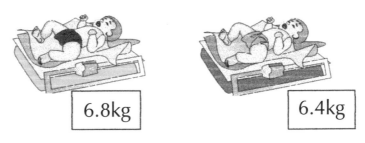

3. Which mini-beast is the longest?

4. Which doorway is the narrowest?

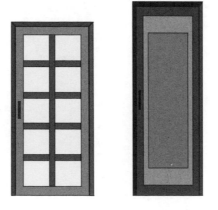

In session 7 you looked at **capacity**.
   Write your own definition of capacity in this box.

Capacity is:

Write your own definition of volume in this box.

Volume is:

Link the word/phrase to the picture.

- Half-full
- Empty
- Full
- Three-quarters empty

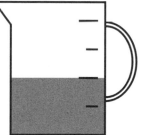
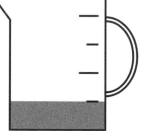
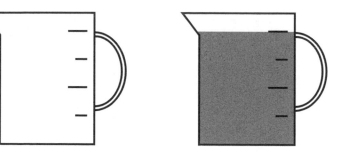

These activities relate to:
Entry level one, session 8

Activity 1

In this session you covered **two-dimensional** and **three-dimensional** shapes, otherwise known as 2D and 3D shapes.

Name the shapes below. Are they 2D or 3D?

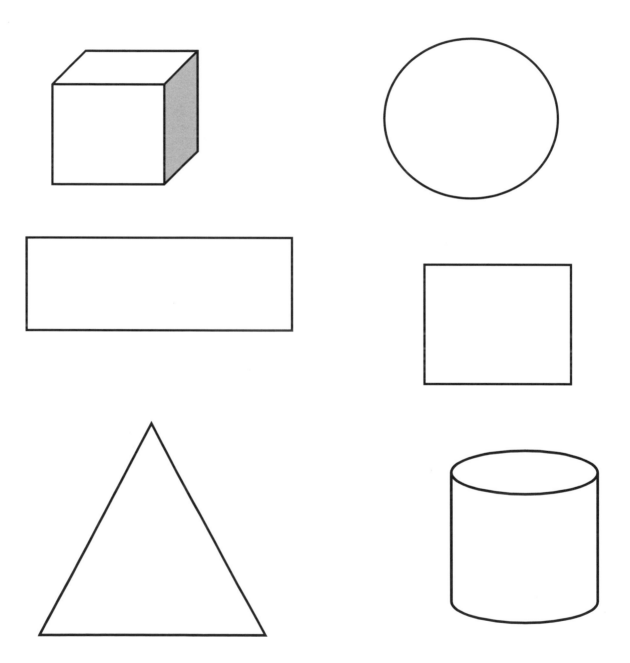

These activities relate to:
Entry level one, session 8

Activity 2

In session 8 you also looked at **positional vocabulary**. Look at the picture below and answer questions 1–5.

1. In relation to the house, where is the mountain?

2. In relation to the window, where is the dog?

3. In relation to the door, where is the woman who is sewing?

4. In relation to the house, where is the cactus?

5. Describe where the chimney is.

This activity relates to:
Entry level one, session 9

Below is a list of school term times for Birmingham.

1. When is the Autumn half term?

2. When does the Summer term begin?

3. When does the Spring term end?

4. List the dates when each term starts.

5. List the dates when each term ends.

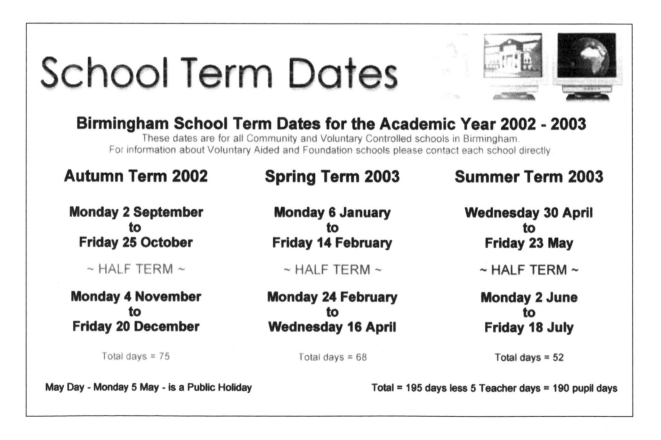

School Term Dates

Birmingham School Term Dates for the Academic Year 2002 - 2003

These dates are for all Community and Voluntary Controlled schools in Birmingham.
For information about Voluntary Aided and Foundation schools please contact each school directly

Autumn Term 2002	Spring Term 2003	Summer Term 2003
Monday 2 September to Friday 25 October	Monday 6 January to Friday 14 February	Wednesday 30 April to Friday 23 May
~ HALF TERM ~	~ HALF TERM ~	~ HALF TERM ~
Monday 4 November to Friday 20 December	Monday 24 February to Wednesday 16 April	Monday 2 June to Friday 18 July
Total days = 75	Total days = 68	Total days = 52

May Day - Monday 5 May - is a Public Holiday   Total = 195 days less 5 Teacher days = 190 pupil days

**These activities relate to:
Entry level one, session 10**

Activity 1

In session ten you worked on **times of the day**.

   Fill in this timetable in relation to the course you are doing at college. Some times have been put in for you. You will need to put in the others.

break-times

lectures

	Monday	Tuesday	Wednesday	Thursday	Friday
09.00 – 10.00					
12.00 – 13.00					
14.00 – 15.00					*placement*

lunch-time

Activity 2

In the circles below draw some clocks to show the following times:

- This shop opens at 10 a.m.
- College starts at 9 a.m.
- This restaurant opens at 7 p.m.
- This shop closes at 5 p.m.
- School finishes at 3 p.m.

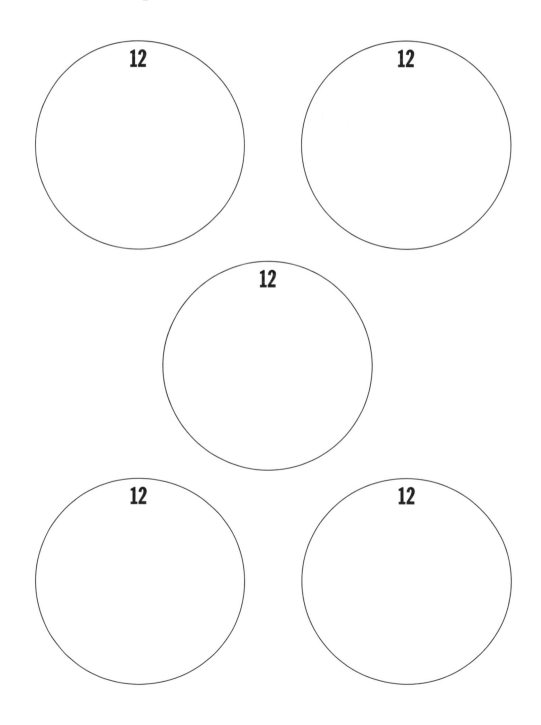

Entry level two activities

In session 1 you worked on **counting** in 2s and 10s.
In the diagrams below some numbers are missing. Can you fill them in?

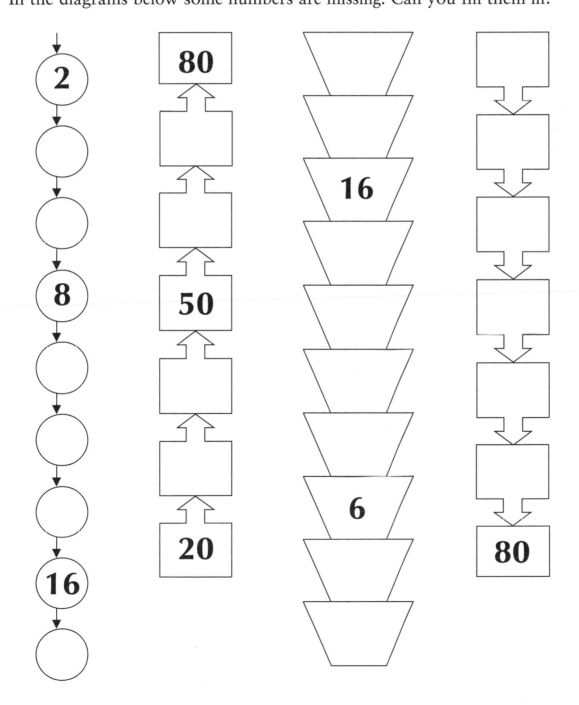

This activity relates to:
Entry level two, session 2

In session 2 you did some addition and subtraction sums in **column format**. Put the following sums into column format and work out the answers.

| 16 + 50 = | 87 + 12 = | 76 + 3 = | 12 + 30 = |
| 30 – 26 = | 65 – 32 = | 45 – 12 = | 22 – 10 = |

In the multiplication square find the answers to the following multiplication sums. The first one has been done for you.

a. 2 x 2	b. 10 x 5	c. 6 x 3	d. 4 x 2
e. 5 x 4	f. 2 x 9	g. 7 x 7	h. 4 x 8
i. 6 x 9	j. 10 x 10	k. 5 x 3	l. 8 x 6

x	1	2	3	4	5	6	7	8	9	10
1	1	2	3	4	5	6	7	8	9	10
2	2	4ᵃ	6	8	10	12	14	16	18	20
3	3	6	9	12	15	18	21	24	27	30
4	4	8	12	16	20	24	28	32	36	40
5	5	10	15	20	25	30	35	40	45	50
6	6	12	18	24	30	36	42	48	54	60
7	7	14	21	28	35	42	49	56	63	70
8	8	16	24	32	40	48	56	64	72	80
9	9	18	27	36	45	54	63	72	81	90
10	10	20	30	40	50	60	70	80	90	100

In session 3 you looked at **volume**.

These activities relate to:
Entry level two, session 3

Activity 1

Lisa is potty training Corran. He used to use eight nappies a day, now he uses only half that amount. How many does he use?

Activity 2

How much do I contain when I am half-full?

How much can two of me hold?

When I'm full I contain 500 ml

How much do I contain when I am a quarter full?

**This activity relates to:
Entry level two, session 4**

In session 4 you looked at different **symbols** used in maths.

- Put the missing numbers and/or symbols in the sums below.
- Use a calculator to work out the answers to the ones without an answer.

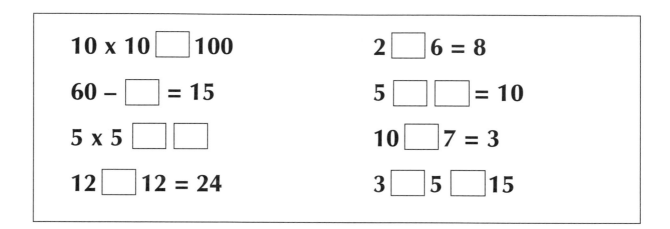

10 x 10 ☐ 100   2 ☐ 6 = 8

60 – ☐ = 15   5 ☐ ☐ = 10

5 x 5 ☐ ☐   10 ☐ 7 = 3

12 ☐ 12 = 24   3 ☐ 5 ☐ 15

- The final three sums are for you to put in the missing symbol of your choice and then work out the answer!

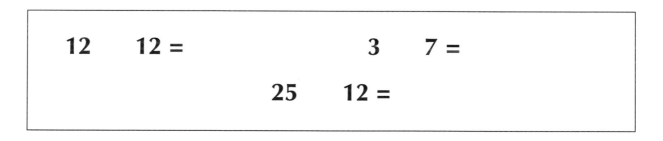

12   12 =   3   7 =

                    25   12 =

In session 5 you worked on **common fractions**.
Write your own definition of 'fraction' in the box below.

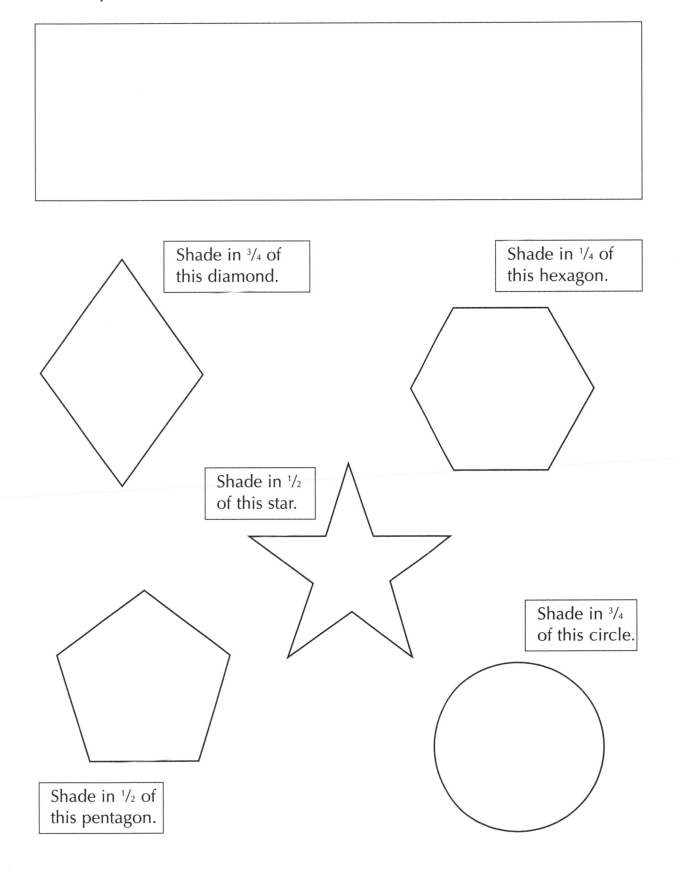

Shade in ³/₄ of this diamond.

Shade in ¼ of this hexagon.

Shade in ½ of this star.

Shade in ³/₄ of this circle.

Shade in ½ of this pentagon.

In session 6 you looked at **currency**.

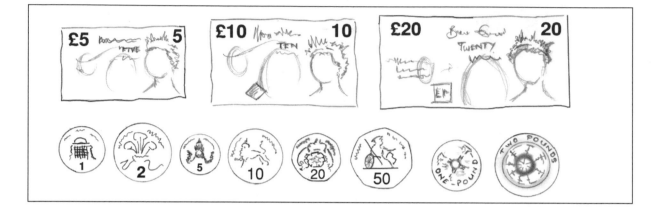

How many ways could you make up the following amounts of money using the coins and notes pictured above:

60p	
75p	
£1	
£1.32	
£1.50	
£6.45	
£12	
£19.99	
£5.45	
£11.50	
56p	
27p	

In session 7 you looked at **dates**.

Activity 1

The names of days and months are shortened by using the first three letters of the name (e.g. Monday becomes Mon and January becomes Jan). There are two exceptions to this, namely September and Thursday, which are shortened to the first four letters of their name.

Years are shortened by missing off the first two numbers.

Fill in the table below with the shortened versions.

Months		Days	
January		Monday	
February		Tuesday	
March		Wednesday	
April		Thursday	
May		Friday	
June		Saturday	
July		Sunday	
August		*Years*	
September		1999	
October		2000	
November		1998	
December		2003	

Activity 2

Put the dates given below into their shortened format:

⇨ Corran was born on May the Fourth 2000

⇨ Radley took his Science SATs on Tuesday May the Sixth 2003

These activities relate to:
Entry level two, session 8

In session 8 you looked at **units of measurement**.

Activity 1

Below are the common units of measurement and their abbreviated forms. Can you match them?

Centimetre	secs
Metre	kg
Millimetre	cm
Kilogram	gm
Gram	mls
Pound	hrs
Pence	£
Hours	mm
Minutes	L
Seconds	mins
Litre	M
Millilitres	p

Activity 2

Fill in the answers to the questions below:

Time is measured in:
Money is measured in:
Length is measured in:
Weight is measured in:
Liquid is measured in:

**These activities relate to:
Entry level two, session 9**

In session 9 you looked at **capacity, temperature** and **weight**.
   Write your definition of capacity here.

Activity 1

Find out the capacity of two football grounds. Which has the smallest capacity?

Activity 2

Take a look at the thermometers below. What temperature is each of them showing?

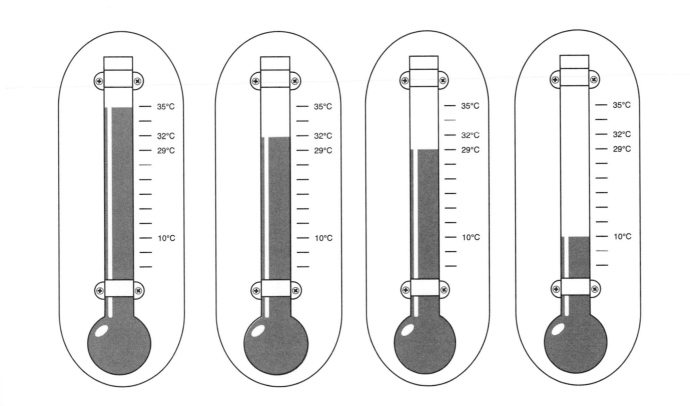

Activity 3

What weights are the scales below showing? What is the heaviest and the lightest weight?

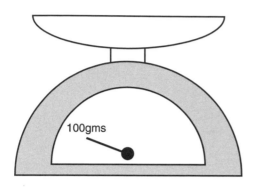

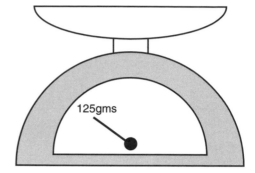

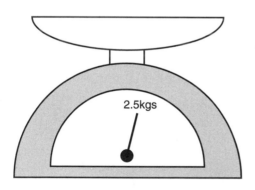

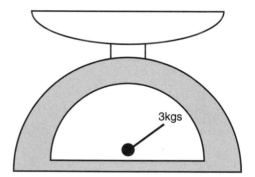

This activity relates to:
Entry level two, session 10

In session 10 you worked on the **properties** of 2D and 3D shapes.

Describe each of the shapes below using words such as corners, sides, straight, curved, 2D, 3D, faces.

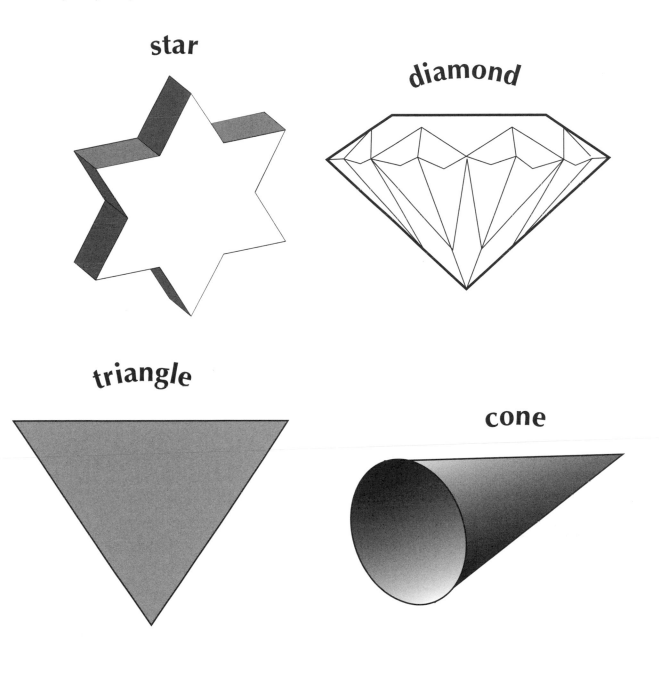

star

diamond

triangle

cone

Entry level three activities

These activities relate to:
Entry level three, session 1

In session 1 you looked at numbers up to 1000.

Activity 1

Match the words to the correct numbers:

Eight hundred and sixty-eight	1,101
	625
One thousand	886
	1,000
Six hundred and fifty-two	868
	652

Activity 2

Complete the following:

326 has _____ hundreds, _____ tens and _____ units

959 has _____ hundreds, _____ tens and _____ units

195 has _____ hundreds, _____ tens and _____ units

Activity 3

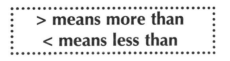

> means more than
< means less than

Use the symbols for more than and less than to fill in the gaps below:

96 is _____ than 82   59 is _____ than 14

89 is _____ than 52   13 is _____ than 26

In session 2 you looked at **estimation**.

Activity 1

REMINDER!
Estimation is making a sensible guess at something based on the information we have.

Take a look at the number lines below. How they are graded is written above each one.

Numbers they begin and end with is the only information you have.

There are two estimations for you to make about each one. Fill in your answer with a dot or a line.

This number line is graded in tens.

10 _____ 100

⇨ Where would 50 be?

⇨ Where would 30 be?

This number line is graded in hundreds.

100 _____ 500

⇨ Where would 150 be?

⇨ Where would 400 be?

This number line is graded in fives.

5 _____ 50

⇨ Where would 30 be?

⇨ Where would 10 be?

These activities relate to:
Entry level three, session 2

Activity 2

Susan is starting her own childminding service. She has to buy the equipment listed below. How much will it cost? Round the total to the nearest £10.

Highchair
£33

Nappy-changing unit
£55

First Aid kit
£15

Buggy
£155

Cot
£95.99

Other items such as nappies, pins, toys, stair-gates, fireguard and other miscellaneous items
£150

These activities relate to:
Entry level three, session 3

Activity 1

In session 3 you covered place value of **decimals**. Fill in the following sentences.

0.4 has [   ] units and [   ] tenths

2.3 has [   ] units and [   ] tenths

0.67 has [   ] units and [   ] tenths

1.2 has [   ] units and [   ] tenths

Activity 2

The square on the right has been divided into tenths. Shade in 0.3.
What is the equivalent fraction?

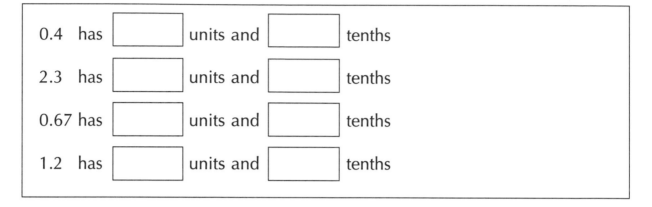

The square on the right has been divided into hundredths. Shade in 0.45.
What is the equivalent fraction?
What is the equivalent percentage?

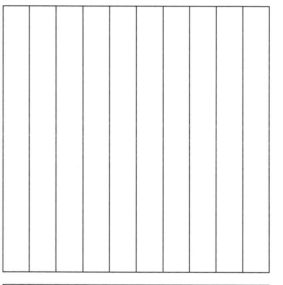

These activities relate to:
Entry level three, session 4

Activity 1

In this session you covered how to **add** and **subtract decimals**. These activities are about adding and subtracting fractions.

The first thing we need to do is cancel the fractions down to the smallest we can.

For example, 6/24 is a big fraction, so we need to find a number that goes into both 6 and 24. The answer is 6, so the fraction becomes 1/4 because 6 goes into 6 once, and into 24 four times:

Have a go at these:

4/8	48/60	16/24	21/49

Activity 2

Adding and subtracting fractions with the same denominator is easy (e.g. 1/5 + 3/5 = 4/5 or 4/5 − 1/5 = 3/5). The way we do it is to add/subtract the numerators and keep the denominators the same. Try these:

6/8 − 1/8 =	3/12 + 4/12 =

Activity 3

If the denominators are different we have to find a 'common denominator'(e.g. 1/3 + 7/12).

Three goes into 12 four times so we multiply the 1/3 × 4 : 1 × 4 = 4, 3 × 4 = 12, so the fraction becomes 4/12. The sum is now 4/12 + 7/12. We add the numerators and keep the denominators the same, so the answer is 11/12:

$$\frac{1}{3} \; {}^{\times 4}_{\times 4} \quad \frac{4}{12} + \frac{7}{12} = \frac{11}{12}$$

Try these:

3/5 + 5/15 =	4/6 − 2/12 =
6/20 + 1/5 =	3/12 − 1/16 =
5/20 + 3/10 =	2/21 − 7/14 =

In session 5 you looked at handling **data**. These activities are based on the information given in the box below.

Annie was unwell when her mum got her up this morning. When she phoned the doctor he asked her to keep a record of her pulse. Below is a list of the times and rates of her pulse. Plot these recordings on the chart below.

⇨ 10 o'clock – 90 beats per minute

⇨ 10.30 – 100 beats per minute

⇨ 11 o'clock – 110 beats per minute

⇨ 11.30 –110 beats per minute

⇨ 12 noon – 100 beats per minute

⇨ 12.30 – 90 beats per minute

⇨ 1 o'clock – 80 beats per minute

Beats per minute		10.00	10.30	11.00	11.30	12.00	12.30	13.00
	120							
	110							
	100							
	90							
	80							
	70							
	60							

☐ Normal rate

1. What time did Annie's pulse rate start to go up?

2. What time was her pulse rate highest and what was it?

3. How much higher was Annie's pulse rate at 12 noon than it was at 10 o'clock?

4. When did Annie's pulse rate return to normal levels?

These activities relate to:
Entry level three, session 6

In session 6 you worked on **right angles** and did some more work on shapes.

⇨ What is an angle?

⇨ What is a right angle?

Here is some more information about angles:

• Angles that are less than 90° are called *acute angles*.
• Angles that are more than 90° but less than 180° are called *obtuse angles*.

Activity 1

Have a look at the angles below. Are they acute or obtuse?

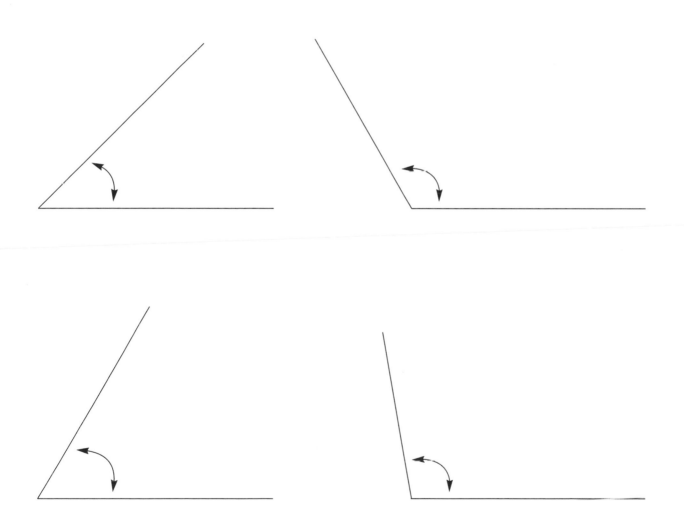

**These activities relate to:
Entry level three, session 6**

Activity 2

Look at the shapes below. In which of them could you draw a line of symmetry?

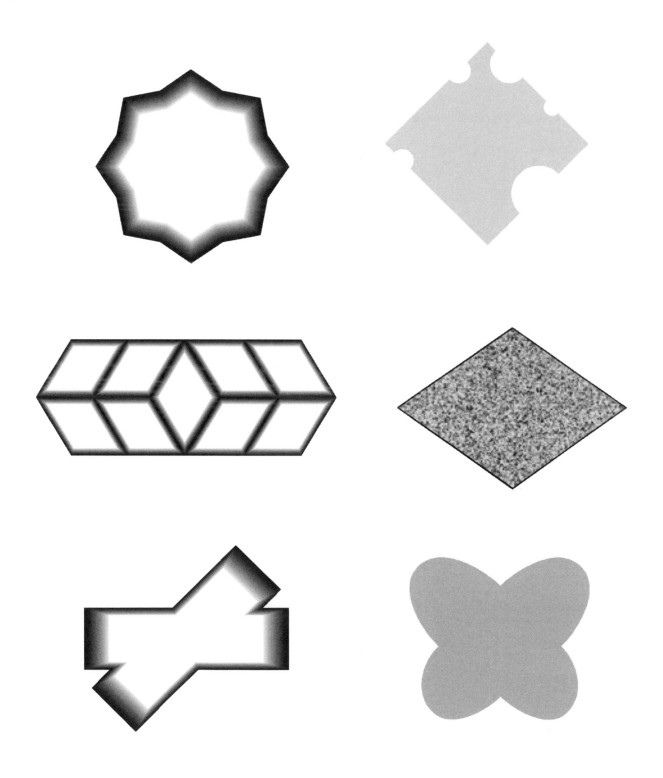

Level one activities

These activities relate to:
Level one, session 1

In session 1 you worked on **seven-digit numbers** and **negative numbers**.

Activity 1

In the number 1,200,262

- What is the value of the 1?

- What is the value of the 2?

- What is the value of the 6?

- Write the number in words:

Activity 2

Put the following numbers into descending order:

3,100,948	2,300,150	3,150,960
2,300,040	3,150,894	

Put the following numbers into ascending order:

6 C   −10 C   8 C   5 C   −5 C

Activity 3

The temperature yesterday was −3 C. Today it is 6 degrees higher.

What is the temperature today?

**These activities relate to:
Level one, session 2**

In session 2 you looked at addition, subtraction, multiplication and division using larger numbers.

Add these numbers together:

- 1,600,750 + 5,600

- 6,780 + 7210

- 2,500,500 + 3,200,500

Subtract 2,300,010 from each of these numbers:

- 3,600,050

- 4,500,654

- 6,300,010

Multiply these numbers:

- $3,000 \times 5$

- $1,200,300 \times 4$

- $7,214,900 \times 2$

Divide these numbers:

- $550 \div 10$

- $600 \div 3$

- $1,200,065 \div 6$

In session 3 you covered **ratio** and **proportion**.

Surj is making fruit salad with the children at playgroup. In each fruit salad there will be:

- five grapes
- six pieces of tangerine
- four pieces of kiwi fruit
- six slices of banana
- three pieces of apple

Below is a table of how many children will do the activity at a time.

Fill it in to show how much fruit Surj will need each time she does the activity.

	grapes	*tangerine*	*kiwi fruit*	*banana*	*apple*
Three children					
Five children					
Four children					

⇨ What is the ratio of banana to each piece of apple?

⇨ What is the ratio of kiwi fruit to tangerine?

⇨ What proportion of the fruit salad is grape?

These activities relate to:
Level one, session 3

In session 3 you also covered **estimation** and **rounding**. The following activities are based on them.

Round these weights to the nearest kilogram:

1. 1.879kg

2. 1.423kg

3. 2.632 kg

4. 6.369kg

Round these lengths to the nearest metre:

1. 1.5m

2. 6.7m

3. 9.09m

4. 5.4m

In the diagram below each square represents $1km^2$. To estimate the area of each playground you need to count the whole squares, join the half squares to make wholes and add them together. Sounds easy!

Try these:

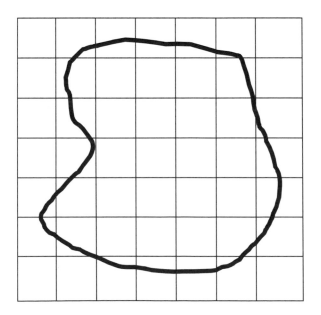
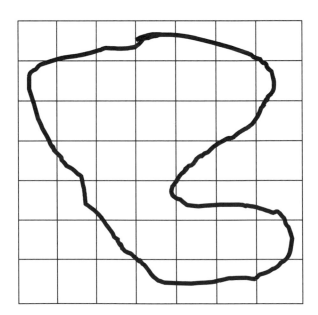

**These activities relate to:
Level one, session 4**

In session 4 you looked at **tessellation**.

REMINDER!

Tessellation is a continuous pattern where there are no gaps between the shapes in the pattern.

Activity 1

This is tessellation. You could add more and more crosses to this pattern.

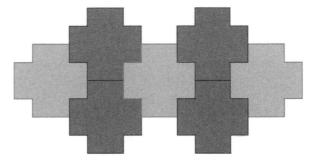

Which of these two patterns is not tessellation?

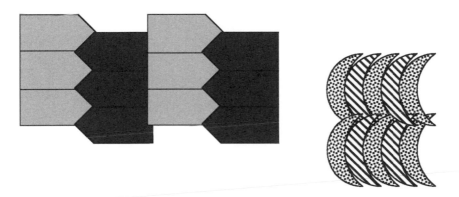

Activity 2

Make your own tessellation using a triangle.

These activities relate to:
Level one, session 5

In session 5 you looked at **time**.

Below is a time line graded in 10-minute intervals.

09.00   09.10   09.20   09.30   09.40   09.50   10.00   10.10   10.20   10.30

⇨ What time is it 20 minutes after 09.30?

⇨ What time is it 40 minutes before 10.00?

⇨ What time is it 50 minutes after 09.30?

⇨ What time is it 30 minutes before 10.20?

This time line is graded in 15-minute intervals.

14.30   14.45   15.00   15.15   15.30   16.00   16.15   16.30   16.45   17.00

⇨ What time is it 15 minutes after 14.45?

⇨ What time is it 30 minutes before 17.00?

⇨ What time is it 60 minutes after 14.30?

⇨ What time is it 45 minutes before 16.15?

More time questions!

⇨ Radley's school day starts at 08.50. It takes him 25 minutes to walk to school. What time does he need to leave home?

⇨ Steve gives June a lift to the bottom of her road, after work. It takes 15 minutes to get to the bottom of her road, then it takes her 5 minutes to walk to her flat. If they leave work at 16.30, what time will June get home?

These activities relate to:
Level one, session 6

In this session you learned about **percentages**.

Activity 1

How much is:

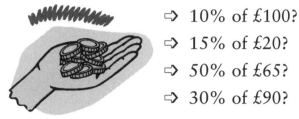

⇨ 10% of £100?

⇨ 15% of £20?

⇨ 50% of £65?

⇨ 30% of £90?

Activity 2

A group of 100 aliens visited earth last week. Ten of them were children, 20 of them were teenagers, 40 of them were male and 30 were female.

Answer the following questions about the aliens.

⇨ What percentage were female?

⇨ What percentage were teenagers?

⇨ What percentage were children?

⇨ What percentage were male?

These activities relate to:
Level one, session 7

In session 7 we looked at measuring area and perimeter.

Activity 1

Measure the perimeter of these shapes:

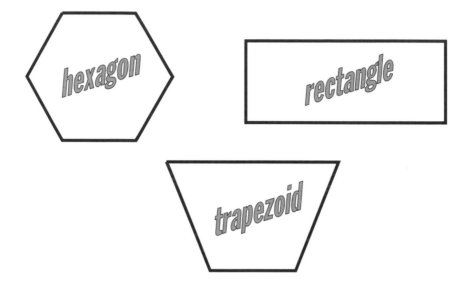

Activity 2

Find the area of these two rectangles:

Activity 3

To find the area of this shape, divide it into rectangles, find the area of each and add them together.

These activities relate to:
Level one, session 7

Activity 4

You also covered **probability** in session 7.
   Try this.

You have two spinners, shaded like this:

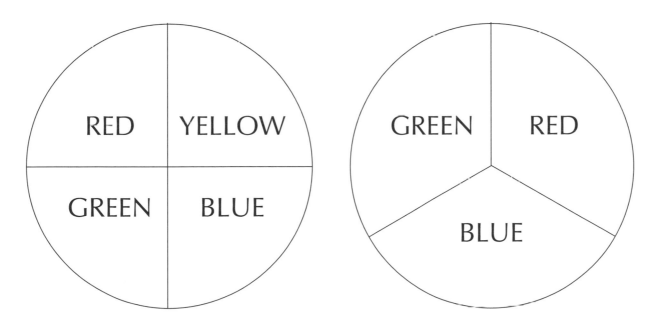

Show all the possible outcomes of both spinners in the table below. It has been started for you.
   Show them in a tree diagram.

		RED	GREEN	BLUE
	Spinner two			
Spinner one	RED		RG	
	YELLOW			
	BLUE			
	GREEN			GB

TO31562

Level two activities

In session 1 you looked at numbers and their properties, and words such as factor and multiple.

Activity 1

What do the following terms mean?

- Multiple
- Factor
- Positive number – give two examples:
- Negative number – give two examples:
- Prime number – give examples:
- Square number

Activity 2

Work out (1) and (2) below. An example is given to help you.

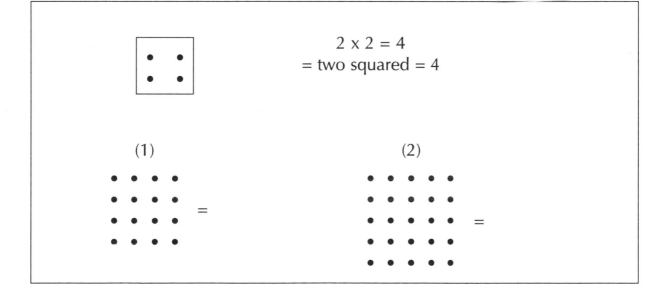

$2 \times 2 = 4$
= two squared = 4

(1)

=

(2)

=

Activity 3

> What is 18 a multiple of?
> What is 20 a multiple of?
> What is 60 a multiple of?

> What are the factors of
> the numbers 30, 9, 16?

> Which of the following
> numbers are prime numbers:
> 4, 2, 3, 6, 10, 11?

**These activities relate to:
Level two, session 2**

In session 2 you looked at **fractions**. When adding and subtracting fractions that have a whole number in them you need to get rid of the whole number first. There are two ways you can do it:

1. break the whole number down into a fraction; for example:

$$1\frac{2}{5} + \frac{3}{5} = \frac{7}{5} + \frac{3}{5} = \frac{10}{5} = 2$$

2. Add just the fractions then add the whole number to your answer.
   Try working out the following:

REMINDER!
When the numerator and denominator are the same it makes a whole (e.g. 7/7 is 1 whole).

$2\frac{3}{8} + \frac{7}{8}$	$1\frac{1}{8} - \frac{2}{16}$
$\frac{1}{10} + 2\frac{4}{10}$	$3\frac{4}{10} - \frac{2}{5}$
$\frac{1}{5} + \frac{3}{10} + \frac{1}{20}$	$4\frac{2}{7} - 3\frac{2}{21}$
$\frac{3}{4} + 1\frac{1}{2} + \frac{3}{8}$	$5\frac{2}{9} - \frac{1}{18} - 2\frac{1}{9}$

As you have done quite a lot of number work already there are no activities linked to Level two, session 3. However, there are some shapes activities for you to do!

Name the following shapes:

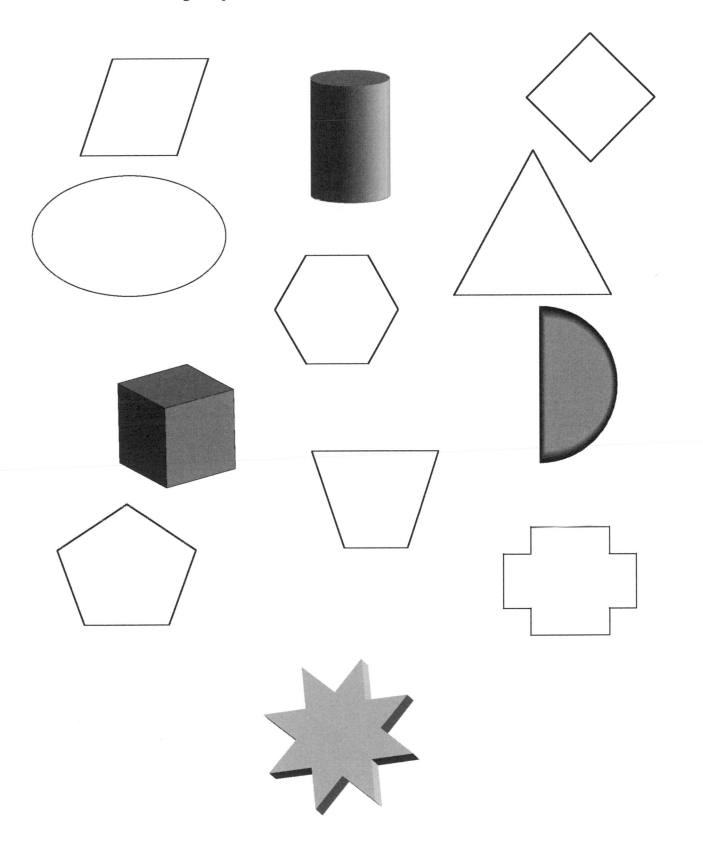

> **These activities relate to:**
> **Level two, session 4**

In session 4 we looked at terms used in data collection.

Activity 1

What is meant by the following terms:

➱ Range

➱ Mean

➱ Median

➱ Mode

Activity 2

What is the range, mean and median of these sets of numbers? Which sets have a mode?

1.	78	33	21	46	94
2.	100	101	64	38	97
3.	29	14	36	28	29
4.	205	600	105	173	182

**These activities relate to:
Level two, session 5**

In session 5 we looked at probability and chance.

Activity 1

At the school fair, there is a bag containing 20 red balls and 30 blue balls. You are allowed to dip in twice. ***Balls are not replaced once they have been taken out.***
   There is a prize if you pull out two balls of the same colour.
   Draw a tree diagram to show the following:

- Chances of picking two red balls.
- Chances of picking two blue balls.
- Chances of picking one of each colour.

Activity 2

Susan bought five raffle tickets at the same fair. One hundred tickets were sold altogether.
   There are two prizes to be won. What are the chances Susan will win one of them?

There are no activities related to Level two, session 6, as you have done a lot of work on dates and conversion, but there are some extra handling data.
You don't get away with it that easily!

While working on tasks to do with handling data you have come across a few different types of data. Two types you have not yet come across are Venn diagrams and Carrol diagrams.

⇨ **Venn diagrams** are used to sort information. For example:

Radley, Chris and Daniel say basketball is their favourite sport.

Damien and Corran say football is their favourite while Jack likes both.

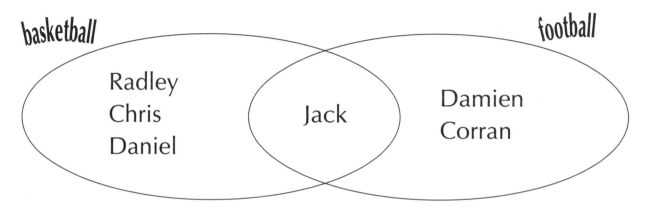

⇨ **Carroll diagrams** are used to sort information in two different ways. For example, here are two shapes, each with two different patterns.

A Carroll diagram can show how many of each there are.

	SPOTTED	STRIPED
CIRCLE	2	5
CRESCENT	4	3

Activity 1

Put the following into a Carroll diagram.

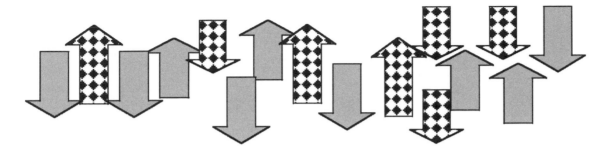

Activity 2

Put the following information into a Venn diagram.

At nursery the children were asked what their favourite activity is. Tom likes painting, Sarah likes playdough, Amjit likes building bricks, Ali likes painting and Tasvira likes playdough.

These activities relate to:
Level two, session 5

In session 7 you looked at **area**.
  What do we mean by:

- 'pi'
- perimeter
- circumference
- diameter
- radius
- volume

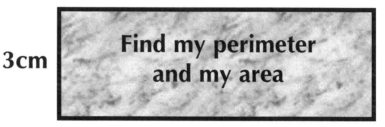

3cm   **Find my perimeter and my area**

4cm

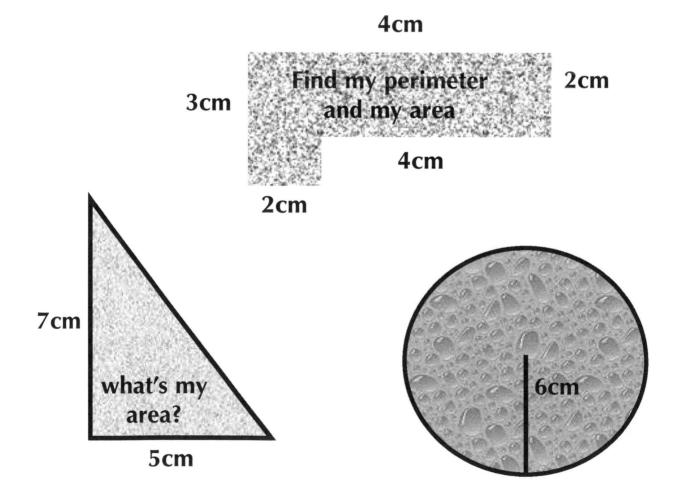

4cm

Find my perimeter and my area   2cm

3cm

4cm

2cm

7cm   what's my area?

5cm

6cm

References

Adult Numeracy

Basic Skills Agency 2001

Cambridge Training and Development Agency (on behalf of the Basic Skills Agency, 1–19 New Oxford Street, London WC1A 1NU)

Core curriculum